ALSO IN THE BLASTA BOOKS SERIES

TANGO

Text by Facundo Rodulfo & Pamela Neumann
Illustrated by Ciara Coogan

CONTENTS

INTRODUCTION

Our journey began in Argentina, a country where life's most cherished moments often revolve around a table. In Argentina, food is more than just nourishment – it's the heartbeat of our culture. Every meal is an opportunity to connect, share stories and celebrate life and togetherness. Whether it's gathering with family or friends for an unforgettable asado, indulging in deep conversations over mate or savouring the sweet simplicity of a medialuna, these experiences are woven into the very fabric of Argentinian life.

Our culinary traditions are a vibrant, intricate mosaic, shaped by the countless immigrants who journeyed here from Italy, Spain, Germany, Poland and even Ireland. Yes, Argentina was once the fifth most popular destination for Irish emigrants and the first non-English-speaking country to welcome them. The blending of these cultures over generations, amalgamated with the ancient traditions of native tribes and the unique gaucho rituals, has given rise to a cuisine that is as diverse as it is delicious, rooted in high standards for quality and a deep appreciation for the joy of sharing a meal.

In 2018, we made Ireland our new home, a country that has embraced us with open arms and provided a nurturing environment for raising our children (four boys, all fans of fútbol, Messi and milanesas!). Here in Ireland, we've found warmth, community and a sense of belonging. But even as we've grown to love our new surroundings, we found ourselves longing for the flavours of our homeland – those tastes and aromas that evoke childhood memories and the comfort of family and friends.

This hunger gave birth to this cookbook, our love letter to Argentina's cuisine. Each recipe is a bridge between our past and our present, and a testament to the power of food to transcend borders, connect people and create community.

This book is more than just a collection of recipes; it's a celebration of the flavours and traditions that define who we are. From the hand-crimped empanadas that bring back memories of family gatherings to the iconic asado that unites people in joyous celebration, these dishes are steeped in the history of our ancestors and the love we carry forward. Yet they have also evolved as we continue to adapt the recipes to the new flavours we have embraced along the way and have made a staple in our daily lives, such as Irish dairy and beef (which we believe are among the best in the world), in the place we call home now.

We hope you'll experience not just the joyful tastes of Argentina but also the deep sense of togetherness and cultural heritage that each recipe embodies. Like the tango – a dance that weaves emotion, history and passion into every step – these recipes tell a story of love, tradition and unity. Whether you're an Argentinian native or discovering these flavours for the first time, we invite you to join us at our table to create new memories and celebrate cultures.

Most of the recipes in this book are from Buenos Aires, our hometown. However, it's important to note that Argentina is a large country with diverse regions, each with its own cooking styles and traditions. While we wish we could include recipes from all these regions, we have selected the ones that hold special meaning for us. These recipes are intended to capture the essence of how they are prepared in Argentinian homes. Some are more complex than others, but all stay true to their legacy.

The best recipes are the ones you make your own, adapting and reinventing them to suit your tastes. Don't just follow the instructions; experiment with the process. Take time to enjoy cooking these dishes and sharing them with your loved ones. Experience the joy of a sobremesa and consider pairing these dishes with a fine Argentinian wine, savouring every sip.

Either way, what really matters is being together, regardless of what's on the menu. Let's celebrate the flavours of Argentina together and, in doing so, create new memories wherever you are. Taste the world and share the love. Let's tango!

PIZZA AL MOLDE
PIZZA BREAD

MAKES 3 PIZZAS

It's said that 80% of the Argentinian population has Italian heritage. This explains our deep-rooted love for pizza and the reason why in many households, it's a family tradition to have pizza at least once a week. While there are many styles, the most popular in Buenos Aires is the pizza al molde: a fluffy pizza that you can cook in your home oven.

One of Facu's first memories is preparing pizza with his auntie, a formidable Italian lady married to a gallant Spanish man from Asturias. Both had migrated to Argentina at an early age. Together, they founded what eventually became a major pizza chain in Argentina (was it Facu's destiny to follow the same journey?). For Pam, growing up in a bakery founded by her parents (her dad from a German family, her mum from an Italian one) meant there was always lots of bread and pizza around – in Argentina, you can buy fresh 'pre-pizza' (pre-made, ready-to-cook pizza) in any bakery as well as at the supermarket.

FOR THE DOUGH:

650g (2¾ cups) lukewarm water

1kg (2¼lb) strong white flour

1 x 7g (¼oz) sachet of fast-action dried yeast

20g (1 tbsp) salt

50g (¼ cup) olive oil, plus extra for greasing

FOR THE SAUCE:

2 tbsp olive oil

1 garlic clove, finely chopped

300g (1¼ cups) tomato passata

a pinch of dried or fresh oregano

We weigh all the dough ingredients for greater accuracy. Pour the water into the bowl of a stand mixer fitted with the dough hook. Add the flour and yeast and mix for 7 minutes on a low speed until it comes together into a dough. Add the salt, then increase the speed to medium and gradually add the olive oil. Mix for another 5 minutes, until the dough is smooth and elastic.

Alternatively, to make the dough by hand, put the flour in a large mixing bowl and make a well in the centre. Sprinkle the yeast into the well, then pour in the water and oil, making sure the liquids stay in the well. Start to mix the ingredients by hand, gradually incorporating the flour from the sides of the well. Add the salt and continue mixing until a shaggy dough forms. Tip the dough onto a lightly floured surface. Knead the dough by folding it over and pushing it away with the heel of your hand. Continue kneading for about 10 minutes, until the dough becomes smooth and elastic.

Shape the dough into a ball and put it in a large bowl. Cover the bowl with cling film and refrigerate for 24 hours.

4

FOR THE TOPPING:

750g (1lb 10½oz) grated mozzarella cheese

fresh basil leaves

The next day, grease 3 x 25cm (10in) pizza trays with olive oil.

Divide the dough into three equal portions and shape them into balls. Put one ball in each of the oiled pans, cover them with a damp cloth so the dough doesn't dry out and let them rest for 30 minutes.

Meanwhile, to make the sauce, heat the oil in a medium-sized frying pan on a medium heat. Add the garlic and sauté for just a moment, as it can burn quickly. Stir in the passata and a pinch of oregano and cook for about 5 minutes, then remove the pan from the heat.

Once the dough has rested, start stretching each ball by pressing it out flat with your fingers. Do this in two stretching sessions with a 15-minute break between each one. Once stretched, let it rest for 30 minutes more. This pizza will be as thick as focaccia – it's much thicker and fluffier than a Neapolitan thin-crust pizza, so don't expect it to be as flat as that type of pizza.

Preheat the oven to 200°C fan (400°F fan).

Spread the tomato sauce over the dough, then bake in the preheated oven for 10 minutes. Remove the pans from the oven and increase the temperature to 220°C (425°F). Sprinkle over the mozzarella, return the pizzas to the oven and bake for 5 minutes, until the dough is golden brown and the cheese has melted.

Remove from the oven and scatter fresh basil leaves on top, then cut each pizza into six or eight slices to serve.

FUGAZZETA
ARGENTINIAN STUFFED PIZZA

MAKES 2 LARGE PIZZAS

Fugazzeta is a cultural icon. Created from the fusion of Italian and Argentinian flavours, it embodies the essence of our diverse culinary legacy. It's unique to Argentina – you won't find this pizza anywhere else in the world. Born in the streets of Buenos Aires from the marriage of Italian heritage and Argentinian creativity, fugazzeta holds a cherished place in the hearts of porteños ('people of the port' – in other words, people from Buenos Aires). Fugazzeta is more than just food – it's a tradition that brings people closer and celebrates Argentinian culture.

FOR THE DOUGH:

650g (2¾ cups) lukewarm water

1kg (2¼lb) strong white flour

1 x 7g (¼oz) sachet of fast-action dried yeast

20g (1 tbsp) salt

50g (¼ cup) olive oil, plus extra for greasing

FOR THE FILLING AND TOPPING:

16 slices of cooked ham

1kg (2¼lb) grated mozzarella cheese

3 large onions, halved and thinly sliced

1 tsp dried oregano

We weigh all the dough ingredients for greater accuracy. Pour the water into the bowl of a stand mixer fitted with the dough hook. Add the flour and yeast and mix for 7 minutes on a low speed until it comes together into a dough. Add the salt, then increase the speed to medium and gradually add the olive oil. Mix for another 5 minutes, until the dough is smooth and elastic.

Alternatively, to make the dough by hand, put the flour in a large mixing bowl and make a well in the centre. Sprinkle the yeast into the well, then pour in the water and oil, making sure the liquids stay in the well. Start to mix the ingredients by hand, gradually incorporating the flour from the sides of the well. Add the salt and continue mixing until a shaggy dough forms. Tip the dough onto a lightly floured surface. Knead the dough by folding it over and pushing it away with the heel of your hand. Continue kneading for about 10 minutes, until the dough becomes smooth and elastic.

Shape the dough into a ball and put it in a large bowl. Cover the bowl with cling film and refrigerate for 24 hours.

The next day, remove the dough from the refrigerator. Lightly flour a clean work surface, tip the dough out and divide it into four equal portions, shaping them into balls. Cover the balls with a clean cloth and leave to rest for 15 minutes.

Preheat the oven to 180°C fan (350°F fan). Lightly oil 2 x 25cm (10in) pizza trays.

Stretch the dough balls with a rolling pin until they are 2cm (¾in) larger than your pizza trays. Put one stretched-out round of dough on the base of each pan, leaving the excess hanging over the edges of the pan. Cover each pizza base with four ham slices, then sprinkle half of the mozzarella on each pizza. Add the remaining ham slices to cover the cheese.

Cover each pizza with one stretched-out disc of dough. Lightly press the two discs of dough together to remove any air pockets, then seal the edges by crimping them together.

You can use raw onions for the topping, but if you like your onions to have a softer flavour, deflame them by putting them in a heatproof bowl and pour over just-boiled water from the kettle, then drain in a colander. Alternatively, microwave them for 1 minute. Mix the onions with the oregano, then scatter them over the top of each pizza.

Cook in the preheated oven for about 25 minutes, until the bases are cooked and golden brown and the onions are starting to char.

Remove the fugazzeta from the oven and allow to cool for a few minutes to let the melted cheese set a bit, then cut each pizza into six slices and enjoy one of the most popular Argentinian dishes.

SAVOURY DOUGH

MAKES ENOUGH FOR 12–15 EMPANADAS OR 1 PIE

You can use this flaky, easy-to-make dough for savoury recipes from empanadas to pies.

500g (4¼ cups) plain flour

100g (½ cup) unsalted butter, diced

1 large egg

200ml (¾ cup + 4 tsp) warm water

1 tsp sweet paprika

1 tsp salt

Put all the ingredients in the bowl of a stand mixer fitted with the dough hook and mix together for 6 minutes on a low speed, until it all comes together into a smooth dough.

Alternatively, to make the dough by hand, mix the salt into the water. Put the flour and paprika in a large bowl or on a clean work surface. Make a well in the middle and put the butter in the well. Slowly pour most of the warm water into the well and allow the butter to melt, then add the egg. Mix the ingredients from the centre out until you form a uniform dough. You might not need to add all the water. If the dough feels too wet, add 1 tablespoon of flour at a time until it no longer sticks to your hands. Knead on a lightly floured surface until it comes together into a smooth dough – this could take 10–15 minutes.

Form the dough into a disc, wrap it in cling film and refrigerate it for at least 20 minutes or until you want to use it (it will keep for up to two days).

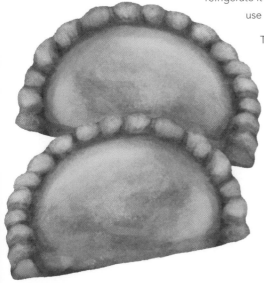

To make empanadas, use a rolling pin to roll out the dough until it's 3mm (¹/8 in) thick. Use a circular cutter with a 12cm (4¾in) diameter (or a similarly sized lid or the rim of a glass) to stamp out the dough – you should get 12–15 discs.

To make a pie, divide the dough into two parts: three-quarters for the base and one-quarter for the top. Use a rolling pin to roll out each disc into a circle approximately 3mm (¹/8 in) thick.

BEEF EMPANADAS

MAKES 12–15

There are entire books about empanadas, and we love them so much that they even feature on the cover of this one. Pietro Sorba defined them as 'embajadoras de identidad, cultura y tradición de cada territorio' (ambassadors of identity, culture and tradition for each corner of the country) and we couldn't agree more. Every region in Argentina (and across Latin America) has its own variations of empanadas, and it's estimated that more than 10 million empanadas are consumed every day in Argentina, which has a population of 45 million people.

1 batch of savoury dough (page 9)

2 eggs

3 tbsp olive oil

1 onion, chopped

3 tbsp sweet paprika

2 tbsp dried parsley

1 tsp–1 tbsp chilli flakes (see the note on page 36)

1 tsp ground cumin

500g (1lb 2oz) good-quality beef mince

1 x 400g (14oz) tin of whole plum tomatoes (we prefer San Marzano)

1 tbsp salt

freshly ground black pepper

120g (1 cup) whole pitted green olives

FOR THE EGG WASH (OPTIONAL):

1 egg, beaten

Make the dough as per the recipe on page 9 up to the point where you put it in the fridge to chill.

Meanwhile, to hard-boil the eggs, put them in a medium saucepan and add enough cold water to cover them by about 1cm (½in). Bring the water to a boil, then reduce the heat to a simmer and cook for 8 minutes. Drain and cool them rapidly under cold running water before peeling and roughly chopping. (You can boil the eggs ahead of time and keep them in the fridge, unpeeled.)

Heat the oil in a large frying pan on a high heat. Once the oil is good and hot, add the onion – it should sizzle when you add it to the pan. Cook for 3 minutes, then add the sweet paprika, dried parsley, chilli flakes and cumin and cook for 30 seconds. Stir in the beef mince and tomatoes and season with the salt and pepper. Break up the mince with the back of a wooden spoon and cook for about 15 minutes, until the beef is nicely browned.

Transfer the mixture to a bowl and allow to cool for about 15 minutes. Add the whole pitted olives and the chopped hard-boiled eggs. Cover the bowl with cling film and chill in the fridge for at least 1 hour (or for up to two days). It's important that the mixture is chilled before filling the empanadas.

Preheat the oven to 200°C fan (400°F fan). Line two baking trays with non-stick baking paper.

10

Remove the dough from the fridge and use a rolling pin to roll it out until it's 3mm (1/8 in) thick. Use a circular cutter with a 12cm (4¾in) diameter (or a similarly sized lid or the rim of a glass) to stamp out the dough – you should get 12–15 discs.

To fill the empanadas, put one disc in the palm of your hand and add a heaped spoonful of the filling to the middle. Be careful not to overfill or underfill it (you'll notice the difference). Fold the dough in half and seal the edges, leaving at least a 5mm (¼in) flat edge to avoid leaks.

Crimp the dough together with the tines of a fork, then twist the edge to form a corkscrew shape – this technique is known as repulgue in Argentina. If you find this step difficult, you can just use the fork to press the flat edges together along the semicircular side. Put on the lined baking tray and repeat with the remaining discs and filling. For an optional golden finish, brush the tops with egg wash before baking.

Bake in the preheated oven for 15–20 minutes, until the empanadas are golden brown. Allow to cool slightly before serving.

VARIATION:
SPINACH EMPANADAS

To make a béchamel, put 200ml (¾ cup + 4 tsp) milk and 3 heaped tablespoons cornflour in a medium saucepan on a medium heat and whisk together until smooth, ensuring there are no lumps. Stir constantly until it comes to a boil and keep stirring until it starts to thicken. Remove the pan from the heat, stir in 30g (2 tablespoons) butter and leave to cool.

To make the filling, steam 800g (1¾lb) fresh or frozen spinach in a large frying pan set on a medium-high until it has cooked through if frozen or wilted down if fresh, then drain to remove any excess water.

Wipe out the frying pan, then add 3 tablespoons olive oil and set the pan over a high heat. Once the oil is good and hot, add 1 large chopped onion – it should sizzle when you add it to the pan. Cook for 3 minutes, then add 3 chopped garlic cloves and cook for just a moment, as it can easily burn. Remove the pan from the heat and allow to cool.

Preheat the oven to 200°C fan (400°F fan). Line two baking trays with non-stick baking paper.

Transfer the onion and garlic to a large bowl along with the cooked spinach, béchamel, 100g (1 cup) grated Parmesan cheese, 200g (2 cups) grated mozzarella cheese, 1 teaspoon salt, 1 teaspoon freshly ground black pepper and a pinch of ground nutmeg (optional) and stir to combine. Remove the dough from the fridge and roll out, fill and bake the empanadas as in the recipe above.

TARTA PASCUALINA
SPINACH & RICOTTA PIE

SERVES 8–10

The name for this pie comes from Pascua (Easter), but pascualina has become a year-round classic. Pascualina graces the tables of Argentinian households and the menus of traditional eateries in Buenos Aires, from bodegones (our local diners) to rotiserías (take-aways) and deli counters, where it shares space with a delightful array of empanadas, milanesas and other sweet and savoury treats. For many Argentinian families, pascualina is a weekly staple and a delicious way to eat your greens. Whether enjoyed for lunch, dinner or as a grab-and-go option, it's both healthy and convenient. So put on your apron, gather your ingredients and embark on a culinary journey to Argentina as we prepare this iconic dish together.

1 batch of savoury dough (page 9) or 2 sheets of shop-bought ready-rolled shortcrust or puff pastry

FOR THE FILLING:

500g (1lb 2oz) baby spinach, fresh or frozen (see the tip)

1 tbsp olive oil, plus extra for greasing

1 onion, chopped

1 garlic clove, chopped

500g (1lb 2oz) ricotta cheese

150g (1½ cups) Parmesan shavings

1 large egg

1 tsp salt

1 tsp freshly ground black pepper

a pinch of ground nutmeg (optional)

5 large hard-boiled eggs, peeled and left whole (see the instructions on page 10 and the tip on the next page)

1 beaten egg, for egg wash (optional)

Make the dough as per the recipe on page 9 up to the point where you put it in the fridge to chill.

Preheat the oven to 180°C fan (350°F fan).

To make the filling, put the spinach in a hot, dry frying pan set on a high heat. Let it cook down until it's just lightly wilted if fresh or cooked through if frozen. Drain in a colander and allow to cool.

Meanwhile, wipe out the frying pan to remove any water, then add the oil and put the pan over a medium heat. Add the onion and cook for 10–15 minutes, until it's nicely golden, then add the garlic and cook for just a moment, as it can easily burn.

Tip the onion and garlic into a large bowl along with the drained spinach, ricotta, Parmesan, raw egg, salt, pepper and a pinch of nutmeg (if using) and mix to combine.

Remove the dough from the fridge and divide it into two parts: three-quarters for the base and one-quarter for the top. Use a rolling pin to roll out each disc into a circle approximately 3mm (⅛ in) thick.

Lightly oil a 30cm (12in) springform tin. Drape the larger pastry disc into the tin, allowing the excess

TOP TIPS

If you use chard or big-leaf spinach, chop the stems and cook them with the onion.

To prevent the eggs from developing a green ring around the yolks (because they get cooked twice), don't be tempted to hard-boil the eggs for too long – 8 minutes will suffice.

to hang over the sides. Press it down into the base and along the sides to prevent any air bubbles from forming.

Add three-quarters of the filling and spread it out in an even layer, then add the whole peeled hard-boiled eggs on top of the filling, spacing them out evenly. Add the rest of the filling, then cover the top with the smaller disc of dough. Crimp the two discs together, making sure the edge doesn't exceed the height of the tin. Brush the top of the pie with beaten egg if desired (some people also sprinkle over a pinch of sugar) and prick the centre with the tines of a fork to allow the steam to escape while it bakes.

Bake in the preheated oven for about 1 hour, until the filling is set and the pastry is golden. Remove from the oven and allow to cool for 15 minutes before releasing the sides of the tin and cutting into wedges to serve.

CANELONES
SPINACH & RICOTTA CRÊPES

MAKES APPROX. 12

Cannelloni is a classic Italian dish that takes on a unique twist in Argentina, where we prepare them using panqueques (savoury crêpes) instead of pasta, a delightful deviation that somehow just works. Growing up, we were fortunate to have our moms and grannies prepare this dish for us. Facu is Spanish/German and Pamela is Italian/German, but the fact that the same method is used regardless of our different backgrounds highlights the important role of the family in preserving and passing down recipes through the generations.

FOR THE CRÊPES:

4 large eggs

480ml (2 cups) milk

80g (5 tbsp) salted butter, melted and cooled, plus extra for greasing

240g (2 cups) plain flour

FOR THE FILLING:

1kg (2¼lb) fresh baby spinach

2 tbsp olive oil

1 white onion, chopped

1 red onion, chopped

½ red pepper, chopped

1 garlic clove, chopped

1 egg

500g (1lb 2oz) ricotta cheese

1 tsp salt

a pinch of freshly ground black pepper

To make the crêpes, whisk the eggs in a large mixing bowl. Add the milk and melted butter, then slowly add the flour while whisking thoroughly until well blended and smooth.

Melt a little butter in a non-stick frying pan over a medium-high heat. Pour in a ladleful of the batter, then tilt the pan to spread it out in a thin, even layer across the base. Cook for a few minutes on each side, until golden. Slide out onto a plate while you cook the rest – you should get approx. 12 crêpes. Add more butter to grease the pan in between batches if needed.

To make the filling, put the spinach in a hot, dry frying pan set on a high heat. Let it cook down until it's just lightly wilted. Drain in a colander and allow to cool.

Wipe out the pan to remove any water, then add the oil and set the pan over a medium heat. When the oil is hot, add the onions and pepper and cook for about 10 minutes, until the onions are transparent. Add the garlic and cook for 30 seconds more, just until fragrant.

Tip the onion mixture into a bowl along with the wilted spinach, egg, ricotta, salt and pepper, mixing well. Set aside.

To make the tomato sauce, heat the oil in a saucepan over a medium heat. Add the spring onion and red pepper and cook for a few minutes, until softened, then add the garlic and cook for 30 seconds more, just until fragrant. Stir in the tomato passata and simmer for 15 minutes.

FOR THE TOMATO SAUCE:

1 tbsp olive oil

1 spring onion, chopped

½ red pepper, chopped

1 garlic clove, chopped

1 litre (4¼ cups) tomato passata

FOR THE BÉCHAMEL:

100g (¾ cup) cornflour

720ml (3 cups) milk

110g (½ cup) salted butter, diced

1 tsp salt

1 tsp freshly ground black pepper

a pinch of ground nutmeg

TO SERVE:

freshly grated Parmesan cheese

To make the béchamel, put the cornflour in a cup and add a bit of the milk. Stir with a fork until smooth, then pour this mixture into a saucepan set over a medium heat. Slowly add the rest of the milk, stirring constantly for a few minutes, until it starts to thicken. Once it has reached the consistency of a thick yogurt, remove the pan from the heat and add the butter, salt, pepper and nutmeg. Mix well until the butter has melted, then set aside to cool.

Preheat the fan to 180°C fan (350°F fan).

To assemble, lay out all the crêpes on a clean tabletop or counter and distribute the filling equally among them. Roll up each crêpe tightly, avoiding any air pockets.

Spread a little tomato sauce on the bottom of two large baking dishes to prevent sticking. Divide the canelones between the dishes, nestling them side by side. It's okay if the canelones are a bit longer than your dishes – the edges can stick up a little. Cover with the remaining tomato sauce, then pour over the béchamel. Bake in the preheated oven for 15 minutes, until heated through and the sauce is bubbling.

Serve with plenty of freshly grated Parmesan sprinkled on top.

ASADO
SLOW-COOKED SHORT RIBS

SERVES 4

The word *asado* refers to the cut of meat but also to the ritual itself when it comes to a get-together with family or friends (there's more about this in the section on sobremesa on pages 42–43). Usually, the words *parrillero* or *asador* are used to refer to the person preparing the asado. You may have heard the phrase 'un aplauso para el asador', which is commonly said after the grilling is done and the food is ready to serve, meaning you applaud the grill master.

Asado is one of the most popular cuts in Argentina and can be found as short ribs or cross-cut steak, usually accompanied by a simple tomato and lettuce salad with olive oil and vinegar, chips or potato wedges, and plenty of provenzal, chimichurri or salsa criolla as dressing. When you think of Argentina, you might envision a gaucho by the fire pit preparing asado. As much as we'd like to include a traditional parrilla recipe, there are just so many factors involved, such as the barbecue set-up, the choice between wood or charcoal and many other variables. Instead, here's a simplified version that can easily be prepared in your home oven.

1 onion, quartered

4 garlic cloves, halved

60ml (¼ cup) Malbec

1–1.2kg (2¼–2¾lb) short ribs, all in one piece

1 tbsp salt

TO SERVE:

papas a la Provenzal (page 33) or chips (page 28)

chimichurri (page 36)

salsa criolla (page 37)

Preheat the oven to 180°C fan (350°F fan).

Put the onion and garlic in a roasting tin that will fit the ribs snugly and pour in the Malbec, then put the short ribs on top. Sprinkle the salt over the ribs, then cover the tin tightly with foil.

Cook in the preheated oven for 4 hours, until the meat is meltingly tender and falling off the bone. Remove from the oven and allow the ribs to cool slightly before slicing into individual portions.

Serve with papas a la Provenzal or chips, with chimichurri and salsa criolla on the side.

TRY THIS

For a smoky finish, grill the ribs on the barbecue for about 5 minutes, bone side down.

PASTEL DE PAPA
ARGENTINIAN COTTAGE PIE

SERVES 10–12

You might be surprised – as we were when we moved to Ireland – that pastel de papa is one of our cherished recipes. It makes you wonder how we can have much in common, even when we're from such different countries. As we always say, food has a unique way of bringing us all together. Take this cottage pie, for example. It's a beloved traditional dish in both Ireland and Argentina, and a true cultural staple. No matter where you're from – whether you're Irish, Argentinian or anything else – we think you'll find comfort in it. We're excited to share our family's version of this classic with you.

4 hard-boiled eggs (see the instructions on page 10)

3 tbsp olive oil

3 medium onions, chopped

1 red pepper, chopped

1 garlic clove, chopped

1 tsp chilli flakes

1 tsp sweet paprika

1kg (2¼lb) beef mince

400ml (1²/₃ cups) tomato passata

1 tsp salt

1 tsp ground black pepper

FOR THE MASHED POTATO TOPPING:

2kg (4½lb) potatoes, peeled and cut into medium-sized pieces

1 tsp salt

110g (½ cup) unsalted butter, diced

120ml (½ cup) milk

1 tsp ground black pepper

a pinch of ground nutmeg

Preheat the oven to 200°C fan (400°F fan).

Hard-boil the eggs as per the recipe on page 10, then peel, chop and set aside.

This is how we make the mashed potato topping, but feel free to use your own family recipe if you like. Put the potatoes in a large saucepan and cover with water by at least 3cm (1¼in). Add the salt and bring to a boil, then reduce the heat and simmer for 10–15 minutes, until the potatoes are tender. Drain in a colander, then return them to the saucepan and allow them to steam dry. Add the butter, milk, pepper and nutmeg and mash together while the potatoes are still hot. Set aside.

Heat the oil in a large frying pan on a high heat. Once the oil is good and hot, add the onions and red pepper – they should sizzle when you add them to the pan. Cook for 3 minutes, then add the garlic and cook for just a moment, as it can easily burn.

Add the chilli flakes and sweet paprika and cook for 30 seconds, then stir in the beef mince and tomato passata and season with the salt and pepper. Break up the mince with the back of a wooden spoon and cook for about 15 minutes, until the beef is nicely browned.

Remove the pan from the heat and let it cool for about 15 minutes, then stir in the chopped hard-boiled eggs.

To assemble, spread half of the mashed potatoes in the bottom of a large baking dish. Add the filling and spread it out evenly, then cover with the remaining mash. Run the tines of a fork along the topping to help it crisp up a bit in the oven.

Cook in the preheated oven for about 15 minutes, until the filling is starting to bubble up around the edges and the topping is starting to turn golden brown.

Serve straight to the table. We like to grate over some Parmesan.

TO SERVE:

freshly grated Parmesan cheese

MATAMBRE ARROLLADO
ARGENTINIAN STUFFED STEAK

SERVES 4–6

Matambre combines two Spanish words: *matar* (to kill) and *hambre* (hunger). Around 1800, Argentina supplied Europe with beef. The meat that seemed useless was the payment to the slaughterers who cut up the cattle and prepared them for later consumption. After finishing their work, the employees lit a fire and cooked the thin meat to 'kill hunger'.

Matambre arrollado is served cold and is a classic dish on the Christmas dinner menu. In Argentina, we gather for dinner on December 24th and wait until midnight to open all the presents. Christmas falls during the summer in the Southern Hemisphere, so we enjoy many cold dishes and stay up late. The same happens on New Year's Eve: we have dinner on the night of the 31st and celebrate with some bubbly as the clock strikes midnight. It's a week filled with food and get-togethers, much like it is in Ireland.

5 hard-boiled eggs (see the instructions on page 10)

1 x 5mm (¼in)-thick beef matambre (see the note on the next page)

3 carrots, grated

2 roasted peppers (try to use different colours), thinly sliced

1 bunch of fresh parsley, finely chopped

1 tsp freshly ground black pepper

100g (1 cup) grated Parmesan cheese (optional)

Hard-boil the eggs as per the recipe on page 10, then peel, cut into large pieces (not chopped) and set aside.

❶ Put the meat on your clean work surface and open it out wide. Remove the layer of fat by carefully cutting and pulling it off (or ask your butcher to do this for you).

❷ Scatter the grated carrots over the beef in an even layer, keeping 2.5cm (1in) clear around each edge. Scatter the roasted peppers on top of the carrots, then the parsley and freshly ground black pepper. Finally, scatter over the chopped hard-boiled eggs. If you like, you can also scatter over a handful of grated Parmesan.

❸ Now you're ready to start rolling. Starting from the short edge closest to you, roll up the meat as tightly as possible while trying to keep all the ingredients in place.

❹ Once fully rolled, tie it with butcher's twine using a butcher's knot, ensuring the edges and centre are secured to prevent the filling from escaping. You can watch videos on YouTube that show you how to tie a butcher's knot.

❺ Once knotted, wrap the matambre tightly in cling film.

Put the tied, wrapped matambre in a large pot and cover with cold water. Put something heavy that can be submerged with food, like cast iron, on top of the matambre to keep it submerged at the bottom of the pot. Bring to a boil, then reduce the heat, cover the pot with a lid and simmer for about 3 hours.

Drain off the water, transfer the matambre to a large plate and let it cool slightly, then carefully remove the cling film. With the matambre still on the plate, put something heavy on top to compress it. We use a large chopping board with a few tins on top. Allow to cool to room temperature.

6 To serve, remove the string and cut the matambre into slices about 1cm (½in) thick.

WHAT IS
THE MATAMBRE CUT?

The matambre cut is a layer of meat found between the ribs of the animal and the skin. It's part of the full rib rack. In the case of beef, the entire piece typically weighs around 2kg (4½lb), depending on the size of the animal. The challenge with matambre is that it can be hard to find this cut outside of Argentina. You can ask your butcher if they can prepare it for you, but you might need to find a suitable alternative. The closest in Ireland would be flank steak, but depending on its thickness, you may need to butterfly it by carefully slicing through the side of the steak so that it opens up like a book, keeping one edge connected to act as a hinge. The result is a thinner, double-sized piece of meat. It needs to have a rectangular shape that's approximately 25cm x 40cm (10in x 16in) so that you can roll it – it will look like a meaty Swiss roll.

POLENTA WITH MEATBALLS

SERVES 6–8

This dish is very popular in Argentina and is one of our boys' favourites. It's delicious, comforting, and quick and easy to prepare. We usually serve polenta with tomato sauce, Bolognese or meatballs at home, but it's also tasty on its own, especially if you enjoy melted cheese. If you have any leftover polenta, try this: shape it into small balls, put a cube of cheese in the centre of each one and deep-fry them for a cheesy bite.

FOR THE MEATBALLS:

500g (1lb 2oz) beef mince

1 large egg

1 garlic clove, chopped

1 tbsp dried parsley

1 tsp salt

1 tsp ground black pepper

FOR THE SAUCE:

1 tbsp olive oil

1 onion, chopped

2 garlic cloves, chopped

1 litre (4¼ cups) tomato passata

1 tsp Italian herb seasoning

1 tsp salt

1 tsp ground black pepper

FOR THE POLENTA:

1 litre (4¼ cups) milk

1 litre (4¼ cups) water

salt and freshly ground black pepper

500g (1lb 2oz) instant polenta

110g (½ cup) butter, diced

To make the meatballs, put all the ingredients in a bowl and use your hands to combine. Form into balls (we suggest 3cm (1¼in) diameter), put them on a baking tray and set aside.

To make the sauce, heat the oil in a large frying pan over a high heat. Once the oil is good and hot, add the onion – it should sizzle when you add it to the pan. Cook for 3 minutes, then add the garlic and cook for just a moment, as it can easily burn.

Add the meatballs and cook until they are browned all over. Stir in the passata, Italian herb seasoning, salt and pepper. Reduce the heat to medium and simmer for 10 minutes.

Meanwhile, to make the polenta, put the milk and water in a large saucepan over a medium heat and bring up to a simmer. Season with salt and pepper, then slowly pour in the polenta while whisking continuously to prevent lumps from forming. The emphasis here is on *slowly*, but you also don't want to take too long, otherwise the milk might bubble up and over the sides of the pan. Keep stirring until all the polenta has been added, then remove the pan from the heat and stir in the butter.

If you have kids at home, form the polenta into a volcano shape before pouring in the tomato sauce and adding a few meatballs. They'll love it!

CARNE GLASEADA A LA CERVEZA
BEER-GLAZED PORK FILLET

SERVES 2

Historically, women typically handled most of the cooking in the kitchen and men were often seen as the masters of the barbecue grill. This recipe is special for Facu because it's the only one his dad prepared in his mom's kitchen. While in Argentina a lager is generally used in this recipe (the most traditional beer brand is Quilmes), we have always preferred to use stout. We've given it an Irish twist by using Guinness, which was our favourite even before we moved to Ireland.

1 x 600g (1¼lb) pork fillet

1 tsp salt

1 tsp freshly ground black pepper

2 tbsp olive oil

200g (1¼ cups) honey

100g (⅓ cup) Dijon mustard

2 red onions, halved

4 garlic cloves, cut in half

1 litre (4¼ cups) Guinness stout

TO SERVE:

mashed potatoes, chips (page 28) or papas a la Provenzal (page 33)

Preheat the oven to 150°C fan (300°F fan).

Season the pork with the salt and pepper. Heat the oil in a large frying pan over a high heat, then add the pork and sear it until golden brown on all sides. Remove from the pan and allow to cool slightly.

Mix the honey and mustard together in a small bowl, then rub this all over the pork.

Put the onions and garlic in a roasting tin that will fit the pork snugly, then put the pork on top. Pour in the Guinness and cover the tin tightly with foil. Cook in the preheated oven for 2–2½ hours, until the internal temperature of the meat is at least 63°C (145°F).

Remove the pork from the tin, carve into slices and serve with mashed potatoes, chips or as papas a la Provenzal.

TOP TIP
You can shred the meat and use it in a sandwich or as an empanada filling.

MILANESAS
ARGENTINIAN SCHNITZEL

MAKES APPROX. 15

Milanesas are similar to Austrian Wiener schnitzel, Spanish escalopes or Japanese tonkatsu. Apparently the origin of the milanesa can be traced back to the 12th century. In the year 1134, Milan was just another city in the Austro-Hungarian Empire, where an Italian chef first presented the dish at the Austrian court. With the arrival of Italian immigrants to Argentina, the cotoletta alla milanese transformed into the milanesa we know today.

These breaded, fried cutlets quickly became a staple, adapting to regional tastes in their multiple and flavourful presentations. In addition to beef, milanesas can be prepared with chicken, fish (surubi or dorado are our favourite types of fish, commonly found in Entre Ríos or Corrientes), pork, ñandú (a bird larger than a turkey that looks like an ostrich), carpincho (capybara) or vegetarian options such as aubergines.

There's more to the story! In the 1950s, milanesa a la Napolitana began to gain popularity and eventually became one of the nation's favourite dishes. Its creation was the result of an accident. Legend has it that Don José Nápoli, the owner of a gastropub located across from the Luna Park stadium in Buenos Aires, came up with the idea to 'dress up' a milanesa that had been burned in the fryer. To disguise it, he added tomato sauce, ham and mozzarella cheese – ingredients he typically used for the pizzas enjoyed by customers after watching boxing matches at Luna Park.

The most important thing for any Argentinian is that their mother's (or granny's) milanesas are unmatched. Even our beloved football legend Lionel Messi cherishes his mother's milanesas, recalling how they provided comfort throughout his career and during World Cups. Our own boys obviously love milanesas too (and adore Messi)!

1kg (2¼lb) thin-cut beef steaks (any kind; see the tip on page 26)

1kg (2¼lb) dried breadcrumbs

5 tbsp finely chopped fresh parsley

5 large eggs

3 garlic cloves, finely chopped

120ml (½ cup) milk

Trim off any excess fat or sinew from the steaks, ensuring they are as clean as possible (if using minute steaks, this probably won't be necessary). If your beef isn't already quite thin, pound it with a mallet until it's 5mm (¼in) thick all over.

Set up your pané station by putting the breadcrumbs and parsley in a large baking dish and stirring to combine. Put the eggs, garlic, milk, paprika, salt, mustard, chilli flakes and ground black pepper in a second large baking dish and whisk together.

Working with one at a time, coat the cutlet in breadcrumbs, making sure it's completely and evenly covered –

1 tbsp sweet paprika

1 tbsp salt

1 tbsp Dijon mustard

1 tsp chilli flakes

1 tsp freshly ground black pepper

vegetable oil, for deep-frying (not needed if using the oven)

chips (page 28), mashed potatoes or papas a la Provenzal (page 33), Spanish tortilla (page 29) or a green salad

don't be afraid to press firmly. Dredge the cutlet in the egg mixture, again ensuring it's well-coated, then coat it in the breadcrumbs again. Put on a baking tray and repeat with the remaining cutlets.

You can freeze the milanesas at this point if you don't want to cook them all. Put a piece of parchment paper between each one so they don't stick together, then put them in a freezerproof ziplock bag. They can be frozen for up to six months. See the tip on the next page for more info on how to cook them from frozen.

To cook the milanesas, you can either deep-fry them or cook them in the oven. Deep-frying is a bit messier and more time-consuming than cooking them in the oven, but results in beautifully crispy, crunchy milanesas.

To deep-fry, heat the vegetable oil in a large, wide frying pan over a medium-high heat until it reaches 180°C (350°F). If you don't have a thermometer, you can test the temperature by dropping a cube of bread into the hot oil – if it turns golden brown in about 1 minute, it's just right.

VARIATION:
MILANESA A LA NAPOLITANA

This is basically a pizza-style milanesa. It's one of the top five dishes for just about any Argentinian. Make the milanesas as above, then put them on two large baking trays lined with non-stick baking paper. Preheat the oven to 200°C fan (400°F fan) – you don't deep-fry this version. To make the tomato sauce, heat 1 tablespoon olive oil in a saucepan over a medium-high heat. Add 1 chopped garlic clove and cook for 30 seconds, just until fragrant. Garlic goes from gold to black really quickly, so be careful not to burn it. Stir in 1 x 400g (14oz) tin of whole plum tomatoes, 1 tablespoon dried oregano and 1 teaspoon salt. Simmer for a few minutes, then remove the pan from the heat and set aside. Spread each milanesa with an even layer of tomato sauce, then scatter 300g (2¾ cups) grated mozzarella over them all. You can also add some cooked ham (prosciutto) as an additional topping if desired. Bake in the preheated oven for about 10 minutes, until the cheese is melted and the tomatoes have browned slightly around the edges. Remove from the oven and garnish with chilli flakes if you like a spicy kick. Serve immediately.

Fry the breaded cutlets one at a time, ensuring they are completely covered by oil. Cook for about 3 minutes on each side, until golden brown. Use tongs to transfer to a wire rack set over a baking tray to allow any excess oil to drip off and to keep the coating nice and crisp. Repeat with the remaining milanesas – you may need to add a little more oil between batches and always ensure the temperature reaches 180°C (350°F) again before cooking the next one.

To cook in the oven, preheat the oven to 200°C fan (400°F fan). Lightly grease two large baking trays with oil. You can also brush or spray the tops of the milanesas with a little oil to give them a nice golden colour once cooked.

Put the milanesas on the trays, then cook in the preheated oven for 12–15 minutes, until they are golden brown and fully cooked through.

Serve the milanesas hot, accompanied by your choice of side dishes such as chips, mashed potatoes or papas a la Provenzal, Spanish tortilla or a lightly dressed green salad. You can also add a generous squeeze of lemon juice or your preferred dressing on top of the milanesas.

TOP TIPS

You can buy minute steaks in most supermarkets or from your butcher. These are ideal since they are already thinly sliced and have little or no fat.

If you're deep-frying milanesas that you've frozen, you need to let them thaw overnight in the fridge first, then pat them dry with kitchen paper to make sure there's no ice or water left on them.

If you're cooking frozen milanesas in the oven, there's no need to defrost them first – you can put them straight into the oven and cook for 15–20 minutes, until fully cooked through. The key, though, is to preheat the trays before putting the milanesas on them so they don't stick.

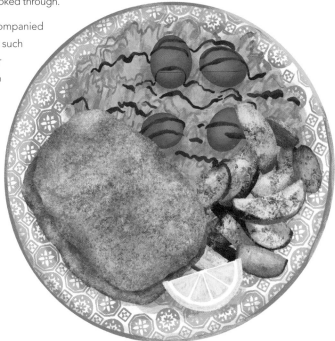

TANGO & STREET FOOD IN ARGENTINA

Tango is one of Argentina's most recognisable cultural exports, celebrated and cherished worldwide. Beyond its global fame, tango embodies who we are and what we aim to share through our food. Tango has set the rhythm of our lives over the last couple of years, especially since opening our food business in Killarney, Kerry. It reflects our desire to bridge cultures through the flavours of our homeland while celebrating the vibrant, diverse nature of Argentinian cuisine.

In Argentina, food brings people together, creating a sense of community and shared experiences. In the past, it was common to see tango dancers performing a la gorra on the streets with a hat for tips while food vendors sold empanadas, bizcochitos or choripanes to the crowds. This tradition continues today in places like La Boca or San Telmo, where both tourists and locals enjoy watching tango dancers while savouring some of Argentina's most beloved street foods. Tango and food capture the spirit of Argentina: passionate, lively and bursting with flavour.

Some of our fondest street food memories are from our time in Buenos Aires many years ago, before we had children. We worked in the area known as el bajo, near the river – Facu in Monserrat and Pam in Puerto Madero. One of the most iconic experiences was grabbing a lomito, a choripán or a bondiola sandwich from the carritos de la Costanera, the food trucks that were lined up along the green reserve by the Río de la Plata. It was more than just a meal; it was a slice of Buenos Aires life served in a bun.

We are arrabaleros (people of the barrio/neighbourhoods), with roots in the working-class areas where tango originated, and street food is an everyday joy. We are passionate and expressive. We wear our hearts on our sleeves, whether dancing, singing, cheering for a football goal or sharing a meal with friends. Tango tells the stories of our struggles, joys and resilience. Meanwhile, street food brings us together in the simplest and most satisfying way. Both embody the essence of Argentina's soul.

REVUELTO GRAMAJO
SCRAMBLED EGGS WITH HAM, POTATOES & PEAS

SERVES 4

This dish is a staple in the Río de la Plata region, particularly in Buenos Aires, making it a classic porteño recipe (porteño translates as 'port city person' and refers to the residents of Buenos Aires). Historians believe it was created by Colonel Artemio Gramajo, who served as an aide-de-camp to General Roca, and the dish is named after him. Today, it's considered a classic comfort food and can be found in most restaurants throughout Argentina. Facu fell in love with it when he first tried it at the age of 15, while for Pam, it was the perfect meal for rainy winter days during her time living and working in Buenos Aires.

3 tbsp olive oil

2 onions, chopped

200g (7oz) cooked ham, cut into thin strips

8 large eggs, beaten

1 x 420g (14½oz) tin of marrowfat peas

salt and freshly ground black pepper

chopped fresh parsley or chives, to garnish

FOR THE CHIPS:

4 large potatoes, peeled and cut into chips

vegetable oil, for deep-frying

1 tsp salt

Bring a pot of salted water to the boil, then add the chips and cook for 3–4 minutes. Drain them in a colander, then pat dry with a clean tea towel.

Heat the oil in your deep-fryer to 160°C (325°F). Working in batches so that you don't overcrowd the fryer, add the chips to the hot oil and deep-fry for about 5 minutes. Drain directly on kitchen paper and repeat with the remaining chips.

Increase the oil to 190°C (375°F). Still working in batches, fry all the chips again for another 1½ –2 minutes, until they turn crisp and golden. Drain again on fresh kitchen paper, then sprinkle with salt.

Heat the olive oil in a frying pan over a medium heat. Add the onions and cook for 8–10 minutes, until softened, then add the ham and cook for another minute. Pour in the beaten eggs and cook, stirring gently, until they are just set (similar to scrambled eggs).

Add the chips and peas and gently toss to combine. Cook for a couple more minutes, until everything is heated through, then season to taste with salt and pepper.

Divide among plates, garnish with fresh parsley or chives and serve immediately.

TORTILLA RELLENA
STUFFED SPANISH TORTILLA

SERVES 8–10

Facu's family on his mom's side comes from Asturias in northern Spain. They migrated to Argentina in 1960 and lived there until the 2000s, when they decided to return to their homeland. Although they were not part of the large waves of Spanish immigrants who arrived at the Buenos Aires port between 1850 and 1950, they exemplify the deep connection between Spain and Argentina. For Facu, this dish is a link to his childhood and his abuelo (grandfather), who raised chickens in the backyard. Facu would collect the eggs for the tortilla, often after getting into some mischief. This meal represents a taste of home and symbolises the love and care that went into every preparation.

2kg (4½lb) potatoes, peeled and cubed

2 tbsp olive oil

6 large eggs

1 bunch of fresh parsley, finely chopped

1 tsp salt

1 tsp freshly ground black pepper

2 onions, thinly sliced

3 slices of cooked ham

200g (2 cups) grated mozzarella cheese (or a mix of mozzarella and Cheddar)

Preheat the oven to 220°C fan (425°F fan). Line a large baking tray with non-stick baking paper.

Toss the cubed potatoes with 1 tablespoon olive oil, then spread them out on the lined baking tray in an even layer. Roast in the preheated oven for 30 minutes, until they are golden and crisp.

Crack the eggs into a bowl, then add the parsley, salt and pepper and whisk to combine. Set aside.

Heat the remaining tablespoon of olive oil in a large non-stick frying pan over a medium heat. Add the onions and cook for about 10 minutes, stirring, until they turn golden brown, then add them to the egg mixture.

Add half of the roasted potatoes to the frying pan. Pour over half of the egg and onion mixture, ensuring it evenly covers the potatoes. Do not stir. Add the ham and cheese, then carefully add the rest of the potatoes and cover with the remaining egg mixture. Cook for 5–8 minutes, until the edges are cooked and the eggs in the centre have started to set.

Using a large plate that's the same size or bigger than your frying pan, put the plate on top of the pan, then carefully invert the pan to flip the tortilla onto the plate without breaking it. Slide it back in the pan and cook the other side for 5 minutes, until the eggs are completely set and cooked through.

Slide the tortilla onto a chopping board, slice into 8–10 wedges and serve immediately. Buen provecho!

GUISO DE LENTEJAS
LENTIL & CHORIZO STEW

SERVES 8–10

This is our favourite stew – delicious, nutritious and comforting. While we would love to include recipes for soups and stews like locro or mondongo, the ingredients for them can be hard to find, so keep those names in mind if you visit Argentina. The vegetables listed here are the ones we use the most, but you can easily substitute them with others, such as potatoes, sweet potatoes, carrots and butternut squash, as long as the quantities are similar. You can also add different legumes or quinoa. Once you've tried this recipe, feel free to experiment and make it your own. This recipe is also perfect for avoiding food waste when you want to prepare a meal with leftover vegetables.

500g (1lb 2oz) dried brown lentils

60ml (¼ cup) olive oil

1 onion, chopped

1 red pepper, finely diced

1 yellow pepper, finely diced

1 garlic clove, chopped

60ml (¼ cup) red wine (optional)

2 x 225g (8oz) rib-eye or sirloin steaks, diced

1 x 225g (8oz) link of dry-cured sweet or spicy Spanish chorizo (we prefer sweet), diced

2 tsp sweet paprika

1 tsp dried parsley

2 tsp salt

1 tsp freshly ground black pepper

1 x 400g (14oz) tin of whole plum tomatoes (we prefer San Marzano)

1 large sweet potato, peeled and diced

1 carrot, chopped

chopped fresh parsley or chives, to garnish

Put the brown lentils in a large bowl, cover with cold water and soak for 3 hours, then drain in a fine mesh sieve and rinse.

Heat the oil in a large pot over a medium heat. Add the onion and peppers and cook for about 4 minutes, until the onion is translucent and starting to soften. Add the garlic and cook for 1 minute more.

Increase the heat to high and pour in the wine (if using). Let it bubble up for a few minutes to cook off the alcohol, then add the diced steak and chorizo. Season with the sweet paprika, parsley, salt and pepper and cook for a few minutes, until the beef is browned. Stir in the drained lentils and the tomatoes, then add the diced sweet potato and carrot.

Cover all the ingredients with water, but don't add too much – it should just cover the ingredients without being excessive. Bring to a boil over a high heat, then reduce the heat to medium and simmer for at least 1½ hours. Ensure the lentils are tender before serving, but be careful not to burn your tongue!

Remove the pot from the heat and let the stew rest for a few minutes. Divide among bowls to serve and garnish with fresh parsley or chives.

POLLO A LA POMAROLA
CHICKEN, PEPPERS & POTATOES IN TOMATO SAUCE

SERVES 4–6

This dish is also known as pollo al disco. The word *disco* refers to an old plough disc that has been ingeniously repurposed by a blacksmith. With added sides and legs, it's an ideal cooking vessel, allowing the dish to be cooked over an open fire. This traditional method gives the dish a unique, rustic flavour, making pollo al disco a favourite in Argentina. The more generic name for this dish is pollo a la pomarola, regardless of whether it's prepared in a disc or a casserole. We're providing instructions for making this dish in your kitchen, but you can try the barbecue version if you're feeling adventurous! This recipe is as significant to Pam as the beer-glazed pork on page 21 is to Facu, as her dad would always prepare it at home, temporarily taking over her mom's kitchen.

120ml (½ cup) olive oil

4 chicken legs

2 large white onions, thinly sliced

2 red peppers, thinly sliced

1 garlic clove, cut in half

3 potatoes, cubed

1 x 400g (14oz) tin of whole plum tomatoes (we prefer San Marzano)

3 bay leaves

2 tbsp sweet paprika

2 tsp salt

1 tsp freshly ground black pepper

200ml (¾ cup + 4 tsp) Malbec red wine

200ml (¾ cup + 4 tsp) water

Heat half of the oil in a large, shallow casserole over a high heat. Add the chicken and cook until golden and seared all over. Remove the chicken from the casserole and set aside.

Reduce the heat to medium, then add the remaining olive oil and allow it to heat up. Add the onions and peppers and cook for about 10 minutes, until softened. Add the garlic and cook for 30 seconds, just until fragrant. Add the potatoes, stirring to coat in the oil, then stir in the tomatoes, bay leaves, paprika, salt and pepper.

Return the chicken to the casserole, then pour in the wine and water. Bring to a boil, then reduce the heat and simmer for about 25 minutes, until the chicken is cooked through and the potatoes are tender. Serve immediately.

ÑOQUIS DE PAPA
POTATO GNOCCHI

SERVES 4

When we lived in Argentina, we always looked forward to having ñoquis at Pam's grandparents' house on the 29th of each month. Her grandmother, Guillermina, made them to perfection, shaping each one individually with a gnocchi paddle. She believed they wouldn't taste the same if they weren't shaped this way. Although she came from a German family, cooking pasta dishes was part of her DNA, highlighting the cultural blending that occurs in Argentina.

In Argentina, the Italian tradition of eating gnocchi on the 29th in honour of Saint Pantaleon is combined with a recognition of the challenges once faced by immigrants in Buenos Aires. Those with limited resources often relied on inexpensive ingredients like flour, while wealthier Italian immigrants would discreetly place coins beneath the plates to help those in need. As a result, it became customary to eat ñoquis on this date and to put a bill under the plate for good fortune.

1kg (2¼lb) potatoes, left whole and unpeeled

350g (3 cups) plain flour, plus extra for dusting

1 large egg

1 egg yolk

1 tsp salt

1 tsp freshly ground black pepper

a pinch of ground nutmeg

butter or olive oil, to prevent sticking

FUN FACT
The word *ñoqui* humorously refers to public employees who only show up at the end of the month to collect their pay, highlighting issues of corruption and nepotism in politics.

Boil the potatoes in a pot of water for 20 minutes, until completely cooked through and tender. Drain and let the potatoes cool.

Once they are cool enough to handle, peel the potatoes, put them in a large mixing bowl and mash them until smooth. Add the flour, egg, egg yolk, salt, pepper and nutmeg and mix until everything is fully combined into a smooth dough.

Lightly flour a clean work surface. Divide the dough into pieces and roll each one into a cylinder about 2cm (¾in) in diameter. Cut the cylinders into 1cm (½in) pieces to form the ñoquis.

Fill a large pot three-quarters full with water and bring to a boil. Add the ñoquis to the boiling water. They will sink to the bottom, then start to float once cooked. As they float to the surface, use a slotted spoon to remove them and put them in a deep serving dish. Add a bit of butter or olive oil to prevent them from sticking together.

Serve the ñoquis with butter and Parmesan cheese, tomato sauce, Bolognese or your preferred pasta topping.

PAPAS A LA PROVENZAL
CHIPS WITH PARSLEY & GARLIC

SERVES 6–8

With golden edges, a soft centre and a touch of garlic and parsley, these delightful potatoes add a burst of flavour to any meal. Whether paired with grilled meats or served as the star on a tapas platter or picada, they are perfect for any occasion that calls for a tasty side dish.

2kg (4½lb) Rooster potatoes, unpeeled and cut into chips or wedges

100ml (⅓ cup + 4 tsp) vegetable oil, plus extra for cooking

8 garlic cloves, finely chopped

1 large bunch of fresh parsley, chopped

Preheat the oven to 200°C fan (400°F fan). Line one or two large baking trays with non-stick baking paper.

Put the potatoes on the lined trays and drizzle with a little oil, tossing to coat, then spread them out in a single layer. Cook in the preheated oven for 20 minutes, until golden and crisp.

Meanwhile, mix the garlic, parsley and 100ml of oil together in a small bowl.

Remove the potatoes from the oven and transfer them to a serving platter. Pour the garlic, parsley and oil mixture over the hot potatoes, tossing to coat them well. Serve them immediately to get the best flavour and texture.

CHIMICHURRI

MAKES 1 MEDIUM JAR

Chimichurri isn't just for steak – it's a versatile flavour booster used across Argentina to spice up everything from potatoes to empanadas and choripán (see the next page). The origins of chimichurri are shrouded in legend. One story traces it back to an Irish immigrant's attempt to recreate Worcestershire sauce. Another tale connects it to British soldiers during a failed invasion, while some credit Basque migrants with introducing a similar sauce. While many claim it's a family recipe, some historians suggest its roots may stretch back to before the arrival of Christopher Columbus, with the word *chimichurri* possibly originating from the Quechua language. What we know for sure is that whether you call it 'Jimmy's curry' or 'tximitxurri', this zesty dip will jazz up any dish.

2 tbsp dried oregano

1 tbsp sweet paprika

1 tsp–1 tbsp chilli flakes (see the note) or 1 fresh red chilli, finely chopped

2 tsp just-boiled water

1 bunch of fresh parsley, finely chopped

3 garlic cloves, finely chopped

4 tsp red wine vinegar

1 tsp honey (optional)

100ml (1/3 cup + 4 tsp) olive or sunflower oil

1 tsp salt

Put the oregano, paprika and chilli flakes or chopped fresh chilli in a medium-sized bowl and pour over the just-boiled water. Stir and let this sit for 10 minutes.

Add the parsley and garlic and stir to combine, then add the vinegar and honey (if using – it balances the acidity). Finally, add the oil and salt and mix until well combined. Refrigerate for 24 hours before using.

Chimichurri can be stored in the fridge in a sealed jar for up to two months. Prepare a batch in the summertime and you'll be covered for a few barbecues.

HOT HOT HOT

Unlike other Latin Americans, Argentinians don't typically enjoy hot food. While we use a variety of spices, our flavours lean more towards Mediterranean herbs. Argentinian chilli flakes (ají molido) are milder than those from other regions, so feel free to adjust this down to 1 teaspoon if you're worried about your chilli flakes being too spicy.

SALSA CRIOLLA

MAKES 1 MEDIUM JAR

In Argentinian cuisine, salsa criolla is a beloved dressing. It's especially popular as a complement to asado, enhancing the rich, smoky flavours of the grilled meat with its fresh, tangy contrast. Salsa criolla is also a favourite topping for choripán, the iconic Argentinian sausage sandwich. Its bright, lively flavour profile adds a burst of freshness and a touch of acidity, balancing the savoury elements of various dishes. Suffice it to say that salsa criolla is a staple in the Argentinian kitchen. Enjoy it with a piece of bread, just as we do.

3 medium-sized ripe tomatoes

1 small onion

1 small red pepper

1 garlic clove, finely chopped

100ml (1/3 cup + 4 tsp) sunflower oil

2 tbsp apple cider vinegar

1 tsp salt

Cut the tomatoes in half and remove the juice and seeds, then finely dice the tomatoes. Dice the onion and red pepper into similar-sized pieces as the tomatoes.

Put the tomatoes, onion, pepper and garlic in a glass jar. Pour in the oil, vinegar and salt and stir well to ensure everything is evenly coated. Cover the jar with a lid and let the salsa criolla rest in the fridge for 24 hours to allow the flavours to meld together.

Serve chilled or at room temperature. This can be kept refrigerated up to four days.

CHORIPÁN

Some butchers in Dublin (and other corners of the world, of course!) are now selling Argentinian-style sausage (chorizo). To make choripán, simply serve the cooked sausage in a panini-style bread or small baguette (the more rustic the crust, the better) with some chimichurri (opposite) or salsa criolla.

BERENJENAS AL ESCABECHE
ARGENTINIAN PICKLED AUBERGINES

MAKES 1 X 1-LITRE JAR

We have a deep love for this pickled aubergine. It can be a fantastic appetiser or a quick snack, especially when paired with your favourite bread or cracker. It's also a perfect addition to a picada before a family meal (a picada is a selection of small plates, similar to tapas). This recipe is a unique blend of techniques from our family and the Ryans, an Irish-Argentinian family we proudly call our friends.

3 aubergines

50g (3 tbsp) coarse salt

3 bay leaves

1 litre (4¼ cups) water

500ml (2 cups + 4 tsp) white wine vinegar

2 garlic cloves, finely chopped

3 tbsp chilli flakes

2 tbsp dried oregano

1 tsp dried parsley

400ml (1²/₃ cups) olive oil (depending on the size of your jar)

To prepare the aubergines, some people peel them, others don't. Some people prefer to cut them into batons (similar to chips), while others cut them into round slices 5–10mm (¼–½in) thick. We leave this up to you to experiment every time you prepare this delightful recipe!

Put the prepared aubergines in a colander and sprinkle over the salt, tossing to ensure all the aubergine pieces are coated with the salt. Put the colander on top of a large bowl to catch the water that drips out, then let them sit for at least 5 hours. If you prepare the aubergines in the morning, they will be ready by noon; if you prepare them in the evening, you can leave them overnight.

Once they've had their rest, you can remove the seeds from the aubergines if you like, but if you're in a hurry or just couldn't be bothered, this step isn't mandatory.

Rinse the salt off the aubergines, then put them in a large saucepan with the bay leaves and cover with the water and vinegar. Bring to a boil and cook for 10–15 minutes, until they look slightly translucent. Thicker aubergine batons or slices will require more time, while thin slices will need slightly less. The texture of the aubergines should be flexible and chewy but not falling apart. Once they are cooked, remove the pan from the heat and allow to cool.

Mix the garlic, chilli flakes, oregano and parsley together in a bowl.

GARLIC
& HERB
MIXTURE

COOKED
AUBERGINES

OLIVE
OIL

Drizzle some of the oil into a clean
1-litre glass jar. Add the first layer
of aubergines, sprinkle some of
the garlic and herb mixture over
the aubergines, then drizzle with
more olive oil. Repeat these layers,
adding more aubergines, garlic and
herb mixture and olive oil until you've
used up all the ingredients and the jar is
full. When adding each layer, press down with the back of
a spoon to remove any air bubbles. Stir it all together, make sure
the last layer is covered with olive oil and add a tiny splash of
vinegar on top if you like an extra pickled taste.

Seal the jar tightly and store it in a cool, dark place or the fridge
(the oil hardens in the cold, so you will need to take it out of the
fridge at least an hour before eating). Allow the flavours to meld
together for one or two days before serving.

BIZCOCHITOS & CUERNITOS DE GRASA
SAVOURY BISCUITS

MAKES APPROX. 75

In Argentina we drink a lot of mate (that small cup filled with yerba and a straw that Messi and the other football players bring everywhere they go) and bizcochitos are the perfect pairing for it. Bizcochitos are quick and easy to prepare, not to mention cheap. These savoury biscuits have been our faithful companions at the most precious 'mate talks', throughout college and on countless beach outings, mountain escapades and road trips.

500g (4¼ cups) plain flour

1 x 7g (¼oz) sachet of fast-action dried yeast (or 25g (1oz) fresh yeast)

160ml (2/3 cup) lukewarm water

250g (9oz) lard or unsalted butter, diced and softened – it must be soft and easy to work with

2 tsp salt

Traditionally these biscuits are made directly on the countertop, but you can use a large bowl if you prefer. Pour the flour into a neat mound on a clean work surface. Make a well in the centre and sprinkle in the yeast. Carefully pour one-quarter of the warm water into the well to dissolve the yeast (you don't need to let it activate first).

Add the diced lard or butter to the well. Use a fork or your hands to slowly incorporate the fat into the mixture in the centre of the well. Start bringing this mixture from the centre outwards while gradually adding the rest of the water until all the ingredients are combined and you form a dough. Add the salt at the last moment, since salt inhibits the yeast. Knead for 5 minutes, then cover with a clean tea towel and let the dough rest for 15 minutes in a warm place.

Roll out the dough with a rolling pin in a rectangular shape and perform a letter fold. To do this, imagine the rectangle is divided into three equal parts. Fold one edge into the middle, then fold the other side into the middle, over the first fold. Let the dough rest for 15 minutes, then roll it out into a rectangle again, perform a letter fold and let it rest for another 15 minutes. Repeat this process one more time. This layering will give a better texture and smoother look to the biscuits.

Roll the dough into a rectangle about 5mm (¼in) thick.

To make bizcochitos, pierce the surface of the dough all over with the tines of a fork. Use a circular cutter (we suggest one that's 3cm (1¼in) in diameter) to stamp out the biscuits.

To make cuernitos, cut the dough into small rectangles about 3cm x 8cm (1¼in x 3¼in). Roll each end of the rectangle to the middle. Where they meet together, overlap one over the other and press them together in the centre.

Once you have finished cutting or folding all your biscuits, put them on two large baking trays lined with non-stick baking paper and let them rest for 15 minutes.

Preheat the oven to 210°C fan (410°F fan).

Bake in the preheated oven for 7 minutes, until golden. These are nice when eaten while still warm, but allow the leftovers to cool completely before storing. They will keep in an airtight container for up to three days at room temperature or for up to a week in the fridge, or they can be frozen and kept in a freezerproof ziplock bag for up to three months. Buen provecho!

THE HEART OF
ARGENTINIAN GATHERINGS

SOBREMESA

Sobremesa is one of those things that's hard to translate, but it means the time you spend together at the table after the meal. It's a way of life that reflects the Argentinian spirit. In a culture where emotions run deep and connections are cherished, sobremesa is the ultimate expression of togetherness. It's a mix of Mediterranean warmth and Latin American passion, where every meal is an opportunity to connect, share and celebrate life's highs and lows.

Whether it's asado, pasta, pizza or empanadas, the table isn't just a place to eat; it's a place to live – to laugh, argue, cry, hug and start over again. It's a reminder that no matter how busy life gets, there's always time to connect with the people who matter most.

When we refer to sobremesa, we usually think of Sundays in Argentina: loud, chaotic and utterly irreplaceable. Sobremesa isn't just about lingering at the table; it's about embracing the messy, beautiful moments that make us who we are as a family.

In Argentina, Sunday wasn't just a day of rest but a day for the family. We'd gather as early as 11 a.m., though preparations often started much earlier. The day began with mate, the traditional Argentinian hot beverage with a cup and straw that you may have seen (we even have an emoji for it!). We sipped slowly as we caught up on the past week and warmed up for an all-day affair. Usually, we enjoyed some medialunas (page 44) or bizcochitos (page 40) from the local bakery that we couldn't resist picking up while also getting bread for later.

Our gathering spot was the quincho, an area of the house dedicated to the art of grilling and socialising, equipped with a large barbecue and an even larger table. The quincho was the heart of our home, where the fire was lit and the conversations began to spark.

As the hours passed, we'd start the picada – a colourful spread of charcuterie, cheese, berenjenas (page 38), olives and crisps, accompanied by a glass of vermouth or the ever-popular Fernet con coca (page 65) – while the asado – an assortment of meats, including chorizos, vacio and entraña – was slowly cooked to perfection over the grill. The air filled with the rich aroma of grilling meats, mingling with the sound of laughter and the occasional friendly (or not?) quarrel over an old family feud while a fútbol match or car race played in the background.

We then commenced with the starters: chorizos, morcillas and provoletas, followed by the mains along with a myriad of salads and the indispensable Malbec. But the sobremesa didn't truly begin until somebody cleared the dishes and dessert was served. The conversations deepened over coffee and something sweet, like a homemade flan (page 52), budín de pan (page 56) or a slice of cake.

We laughed, we cried, we argued and we made up, all within the span of a few hours. And when the weather allowed, some bathed in the sun and shared stories over another round of mate and bizcochitos or medialunas while others napped. Nobody was counting calories, as this was the moment we had been waiting for all week.

Before we knew it, eight hours had passed and it was time to prepare for Monday. But those hours were more than just time spent. They were memories made, bonds strengthened and a testament to the importance of sharing life's moments with those we love.

MEDIALUNAS DE MANTECA
ARGENTINIAN CROISSANTS

MAKES 15

Growing up, Pam spent countless hours in her family's bakery, where the aroma of freshly baked medialunas was a daily delight. These buttery, crescent-shaped pastries are a beloved ritual that brings people together. Whether enjoying them with mate at home, sharing them with friends after a night out (yes, that's a thing!) or savouring them while watching a fútbol match, medialunas are always a part of the moment. Even coffee is incomplete without them. When you go to a cafetería, the menu is 'Café con Leche + Medialuna', and the full experience is to soak the medialunas in the rich, frothy coffee. Today, despite living far from Argentina, Facundo continues the tradition by preparing medialunas for our boys.

500g (4¼ cups) strong white flour

55g (¼ cup) Demerara sugar

1 large egg

1 x 7g (¼oz) sachet of fast-action dried yeast

1 tbsp honey

180ml (¾ cup) water

3 tbsp milk

300g (10½oz) cold salted butter, cut into thin slices

FOR THE EGG WASH:

1 egg, beaten

FOR THE SYRUP:

110g (½ cup) Demerara sugar

120ml (½ cup) water

the peel of 1 orange

1 tbsp honey

Put the flour, sugar, egg, yeast, honey, water and milk in the bowl of a stand mixer fitted with the dough hook. Mix together on a medium speed for about 8 minutes, until combined into a smooth, elastic dough.

Remove the dough from the mixer and put it on a lightly floured surface. Cover with a clean cloth and let it rest for 10 minutes.

Using a rolling pin, stretch the dough into a rectangle about 5mm (¼in) thick. Put the butter slices on two-thirds of the dough, covering it from left to right. Fold the uncovered third of the dough over the middle, then fold again to the left. This creates three layers of dough with butter between each layer. Roll out the dough again to form another rectangle. Fold it again in the same way (from right to left), then put it on a baking tray and refrigerate for 30 minutes.

Preheat the oven to 180°C fan (350°F fan). Line two large baking trays with non-stick baking paper.

After chilling, roll the dough once more into a rectangle about 5mm (¼in) thick, then cut the dough into triangles roughly 8cm x 12cm (3¼in x 4¾in) – you should get 15 triangles. Starting at the base of each triangle, roll the dough towards the tip to create a half-moon crescent shape (the word 'medialuna' means 'half-moon').

44

Put the pastries on the lined trays, then brush the tops with the egg wash for a glossy finish. Bake in the preheated oven for 15 minutes, until golden brown.

Meanwhile, to make the syrup, put the sugar, water, orange peel and honey in a saucepan and bring to a boil, then continue to boil for 5 minutes.

Remove the pastries from the oven and brush with the syrup. Enjoy with coffee or tea.

MEDIALUNAS

SCONES DE CREMA

SCONES DE CREMA
CREAM SCONES

MAKES 15

Scones may not be as popular in Argentina as they are in Ireland, but they are a common item in bakeries, likely a legacy from Irish and British immigrants. A freshly baked scone, served hot while enjoying a cup of tea with family or friends, is one of life's simple pleasures. In addition to being a perfect complement to a hot drink, scones have also been adapted to go with meals as a sweet or savoury option to replace soft breads and in a variety of other creative ways, showcasing their versatility.

400g (3 1/3 cups) plain flour

60g (¼ cup) caster sugar

1 tsp baking soda

100g (½ cup) salted butter, cut into thin slices

1 large egg

200ml (¾ cup + 4 tsp) cream

TO SERVE:

dulce de leche (page 48), Nutella or whipped cream

Put the flour, sugar and baking soda in the bowl of a stand mixer fitted with the paddle attachment and mix to combine. Add the butter, increase the speed to medium and mix until the butter is well combined with the dry ingredients.

Crack in the egg and pour in the cream, then mix on a medium speed again until it all comes together into a uniform dough. Remove the dough from the bowl, form it into a ball, wrap it in cling film and refrigerate for 30 minutes.

Preheat the oven to 200°C fan (400°F fan). Line a large baking tray with non-stick baking paper.

After chilling, roll out the dough until it's 3cm (1¼in) thick. Using a circular cutter with a 5cm (2in) diameter, stamp out about 15 scones and put them on the lined tray, spaced slightly apart.

Bake in the preheated oven for 10–13 minutes, until the scones are well risen and golden brown.

Cut in half and serve with dulce de leche, Nutella or whipped cream.

TORTA DE MANZANA INVERTIDA
UPSIDE-DOWN APPLE CAKE

SERVES 8

We would enjoy a slice of this cake, still warm from the oven, every time we visited Pam's grandparents. Her auntie is the official baker in the family, and we could never resist stopping by to get a slice of whatever she had prepared that day, not to mention our eagerly awaited annual birthday cakes, which each family member requests according to their preferences. This one is dedicated to Susy.

FOR THE CARAMEL APPLE TOPPING:

250g (1¼ cups) caster sugar

1 green apple, halved, cored and thinly sliced

1 red apple, halved, cored and thinly sliced

FOR THE SPONGE CAKE:

200g (1²/₃ cups) self-raising flour

200g (1 cup) caster sugar

5 large eggs

100ml (¹/₃ cup + 4 tsp) milk

1 tsp vanilla extract

Preheat the oven to 180°C fan (350°F fan).

Start by making the caramel. Pour a small quantity of the sugar into a heavy-based frying pan, spreading it evenly to cover the base of the pan. Put the pan over a medium-low heat. Do not stir. As the sugar melts, add another 'layer' of sugar, allowing it to melt completely before adding more. Continue adding the sugar in layers and letting it melt each time so that it melts evenly and doesn't form lumps.

Once all the sugar has been added, stir continuously until the sugar turns a deep amber colour. Quickly pour the caramel into a large non-stick Bundt tin, swirling to coat the bottom evenly and up the sides a bit. Carefully add the apple slices (you don't want to get burned by the hot caramel), sticking them to the caramel on the bottom and sides of the tin. Set aside.

To make the sponge cake, put all the ingredients in the bowl of a stand mixer fitted with the paddle attachment. Mix on a high speed for 3 minutes, then carefully add the batter on top of the caramel and apples.

Bake in the preheated oven for about 35 minutes, until a skewer inserted into the centre comes out clean. Once you remove it from the oven, you must unmould it immediately and transfer it to a serving plate while the caramel is hot, otherwise it will stick and be impossible to remove.

DULCE DE LECHE
MILK CARAMEL

MAKES APPROX. 1 LITRE (4¼ CUPS)

Dulce de leche is the king of ingredients in Argentinian sweets and desserts. Dulce de leche translates to 'milk caramel', but it's not butter caramel or toffee, although it's an excellent alternative to either. It's made by slowly heating sweetened milk until it thickens and turns a caramel colour.

Dulce de leche transports us back to childhood memories of a delicious alfajor (page 50), a scrumptious ice cream (opposite) or toast spread with butter and dulce de leche (we used to call these barquitos, which means 'little boats'), which was especially appreciated on cold mornings with a hot beverage, but also as an afternoon snack after a day at the beach.

We use it to cover desserts or as a sweet filling, or we simply eat it one spoonful at a time. Argentinians love dulce de leche so much, we wouldn't be surprised if there were dulce de leche-scented soaps, candles or shampoo. According to statistics, dulce de leche is the fourth most consumed dairy product in Latin American countries, especially in Argentina, where we claim it as our own creation.

You can buy dulce de leche in the shops but it's easy to make it yourself, either completely from scratch or using tins of condensed milk as a shortcut. The longer you let it cook, the thicker it will be.

FOR THE TRADITIONAL METHOD:

1 litre (4¼ cups) milk

250g (1¼ cups) caster sugar

1 tsp baking soda

1 tsp vanilla extract

FOR THE SHORTCUT:

tins of condensed milk

For the traditional method, put all the ingredients in a heavy-based pot and bring to a boil, stirring constantly. Once the sugar has dissolved, reduce the heat to low and simmer for 4–6 hours, stirring occasionally, until the mixture thickens and turns golden brown.

For a quicker option, use tins of condensed milk. Remove the paper label but leave the tins unopened. Put the tins in a large pot, ensuring they are completely submerged by at least 5cm (2in) of water. Cover the pot with a lid and bring the water to a boil, then keep it boiling for at least 4 hours. The tins need to remain covered with water throughout, so top it up if needed. After 4 hours, remove the pot from the heat and let the tins cool in the water. When opened, the contents should be golden brown and thick.

Or for the easiest method of all, put the sealed tins in a slow cooker, fill the slow cooker with water, cover with the lid and cook on low for 8 hours.

HELADO DE DULCE DE LECHE
DULCE DE LECHE ICE CREAM

SERVES 8–10

Helado de dulce de leche holds a special place in the hearts of Argentinians. It's not just a simple dessert; it's pure comfort and joy. In Argentina, you buy ice cream by the kilo. You can even order it for delivery during extended hours. There are so many flavour combinations that work with dulce de leche, such as banana split (banana, dulce de leche and chocolate shavings), dulce de leche granizado (dulce de leche with chocolate shavings), combining dulce de leche ice cream with fresh dulce de leche, meringue or cookies … we could go on all day!

This luscious, caramel-flavoured ice cream captures the essence of Argentinian indulgence. It's enjoyed at family gatherings, savoured during warm summer evenings and remembered as a comforting taste of home for many Argentinians living abroad.

400g (14oz) dulce de leche (opposite), plus extra to serve

100ml (1/3 cup + 4 tsp) milk

400ml (12/3 cups) double cream

200g (1 cup) chocolate chips, plus extra to serve (optional)

Patience is key in creating this delicious dessert. Mix the dulce de leche with the milk in a large bowl, stirring well until thoroughly combined and smooth.

In a separate bowl, whip the cream until it's thickened but still slightly pourable. Add the whipped cream to the dulce de leche mixture, blending slowly and gently to integrate them without overmixing until you achieve a golden, creamy texture. If desired, stir in the chocolate chips.

Transfer to a freezerproof container and put in the freezer for 2 hours. Stir and freeze again, keeping in mind that the longer you wait, the better it will taste, so freeze it for at least 6 more hours before serving.

To make this even more decadent, you can drizzle some extra dulce de leche on top of each portion and scatter over a few more chocolate chips.

ALFAJORES DE CHOCOLATE
CHOCOLATE ALFIES

MAKES 12

Alfajores are the most popular sweet snack in Argentina. It's calculated that close to 10 million are sold every day. Every region proudly claims its own favourite. There's even an annual championship to crown the best alfajor in the country. Among the most iconic brands is Havanna, which was born in Mar del Plata, the cherished summer holiday destination for Argentinians (when jumping on a flight was not a common thing to do). The factory was just across from the beach, so as you strolled along the promenade, the rich aroma of chocolate would fill the air, creating memories that lingered long after the summer days had passed. The treat was a mandatory souvenir when returning from holidays, and even today, it remains one of the most requested gifts that any expat will ask their friends or family to bring when visiting.

FOR THE COOKIES:

340g (2¾ cups) self-rising flour, plus extra for dusting

170g (1¼ cups) cornflour

60g (½ cup) dark cocoa powder

300g (10½oz) salted butter, diced into small pieces

150g (¾ cup) caster sugar

2 large eggs

2 tbsp honey

FOR THE FILLING:

450g (1lb) dulce de leche (page 48 or shop-bought)

FOR THE COATING:

800g (1¾lb) good-quality chocolate (we suggest a mix of half dark chocolate and half milk chocolate), chopped into small pieces

To make the cookies, put the flour, cornflour and cocoa in a large mixing bowl and whisk to combine.

Put the butter and sugar in the bowl of a stand mixer fitted with the paddle attachment and beat on a high speed until smooth. Add the eggs and honey and continue to beat together until fully incorporated.

Reduce the speed to medium and gradually add the dry ingredients, mixing slowly until just combined, being careful not to overmix. Remove the dough from the bowl, shape it into a flat disc and wrap it in cling film, then refrigerate for 30 minutes.

Preheat the oven to 160°C fan (325°F fan). Line two large baking trays with non-stick baking paper.

Roll out the chilled dough on a lightly floured countertop until it's about 5mm (¼in) thick. Stamp the dough into circles using a cutter that's 5cm (2in) in diameter. You can use a smaller cutter to make smaller, cuter alfajores, but it will take more time to coat them all in the chocolate.

Put the cookies on the lined trays, spaced slightly apart, and bake in the preheated oven for 15 minutes. Allow to cool completely on wire racks for at least 1 hour.

To assemble, spoon the dulce de leche into a piping bag fitted with a plain nozzle. Pipe the dulce de leche onto half of the cookies – the filling should be about 1cm (½in) high. Put the remaining cookies on top to form sandwiches, pressing down gently to avoid breaking them. Use an offset spatula to smooth the surfaces on the sides, making sure there are no air pockets between the cookies and the filling. This will aid in the coating process.

Put the cookie sandwiches on a baking tray and chill them in the fridge while you prepare the chocolate coating.

Line another baking tray with non-stick baking paper and set aside.

Put the chocolate in a heatproof bowl set over a pan of gently simmering water (a bain-marie), making sure the water doesn't touch the bottom of the bowl. Allow the chocolate to melt fully, then remove the bowl from the pan.

Working with one at a time, fully submerge each alfajor into the melted chocolate. Once it's fully coated, put it on the lined tray to let the coating dry and harden. These can be stored in an airtight container in a cool, dark place for up to a week.

DOÑA PETRONA'S FLAN

SERVES 10–12

In the vibrant world of Argentinian cuisine, few names resonate like Doña Petrona's. Her legacy stirs a warm sense of nostalgia and deep admiration, weaving together the diverse threads of culinary tradition throughout the country. She is Argentina's culinary matriarch and her recipes have been passed down through families for generations. From the bustling streets of Buenos Aires to the tranquil pampas, her influence is felt in every corner of our passionate nation. Over her seven-decades-long career, Doña Petrona was a highly influential figure for Argentinian housewives. Just as many Americans fondly recall the dishes prepared from Julia Child's iconic cookbook, *Mastering the Art of French Cooking*, Argentinians have grown up with the cherished flavours of Doña Petrona's recipes. One of her classics is Argentinian flan, a dessert that reminds us of our Spanish roots and culinary traditions. When it comes to making it, Doña Petrona's recipe is the best.

FOR THE CARAMEL:

250g (1¼ cups) caster sugar

FOR THE CUSTARD:

500ml (2 cups + 4 tsp) milk

7 large eggs

200g (¾ cup) caster sugar

1 tsp vanilla extract

TO SERVE:

dulce de leche (page 48)

whipped cream

You will need a large, non-stick Bundt tin or you could use two medium moulds or individual ramekins.

Start by making the caramel. Pour a small quantity of the sugar into a heavy-based frying pan, spreading it evenly to cover the base of the pan. Put the pan over a medium-low heat. Do not stir. As the sugar melts, add another 'layer' of sugar, allowing it to melt completely before adding more. Continue adding the sugar in layers and letting it melt each time so that it melts evenly and doesn't form lumps.

Once all the sugar has been added, stir continuously until the sugar turns a deep amber colour. Some people prefer the caramel to be 'burnt' for a bitter taste. If you like this too, just leave it for a few extra minutes for a darker colour.

Quickly pour the caramel into the Bundt tin or divide it among two moulds or individual ramekins, swirling to coat the bottom(s) evenly. Allow the caramel to cool and harden.

Preheat the oven to 180°C fan (350°F fan).

To make the custard, heat the milk in a saucepan until it's warm but not boiling.

Crack the eggs into a large mixing bowl and whisk together, then slowly add the sugar. Beat the mixture until it's well combined and slightly frothy, then add the vanilla and mix thoroughly.

Gradually pour the warm milk into the egg and sugar mixture while stirring continuously (stir, don't mix!) so that the eggs don't scramble. Strain this custard through a fine mesh sieve, then pour it over the caramel in the Bundt tin, moulds or ramekins.

Put the filled Bundt tin, moulds or ramekins in a deep roasting tin. You can also put a clean cloth in the bottom of the tin to prevent the Bundt tin, moulds or ramekins from slipping or moving. Fill the roasting tin with hot water until it comes about halfway up the sides of the Bundt tin, moulds or ramekins. This water bath helps the flan to cook evenly. Cover the top of the tray tightly with a sheet of foil.

Bake in the preheated oven for 40–45 minutes, until the flan is golden on top and is set but still slightly jiggly in the centre. Check it once or twice during the cooking time to make sure the water doesn't evaporate, adding more if needed.

Remove the flan from the oven and let it cool to room temperature in the water bath, then refrigerate it for at least 4 hours, until it's completely chilled. Bear in mind this recipe is for a large flan to share with family or friends (it makes at least 10 portions), but don't worry – flan can be kept refrigerated for up to four days.

To serve, run a silicone spatula around the edge of the flan to loosen it from the Bundt tin, moulds or ramekins. Put a serving plate on top and quickly invert it to release the flan.

Serve with a generous spoonful of dulce de leche and some whipped cream.

WHAT IS THE TANGO?

Tango isn't just music and dance; it's a lifestyle, a cultural expression that embodies the spirit of Argentina. Originating in the neighbourhoods of Buenos Aires, tango reflects the city's diverse history and emotional depth. It even has its own unique language, lunfardo, a vibrant, expressive slang that has become a defining aspect of Argentinian Spanish, further enhancing the connection to this passionate culture.

BUDÍN DE PAN
BREAD PUDDING

SERVES 10–12

Argentinian-style bread pudding, like its European counterpart, originated as a way to use up stale bread. Due to its low cost, it was initially considered a dessert for the lower classes. However, it has since become a classic dish enjoyed in both restaurants and homes. It's typically served with a generous amount of whipped cream and dulce de leche.

This pudding was a childhood staple for Pam, as her mother often prepared it. There was even a light-hearted disagreement about it among her family members, with some preferring the sweeter caramel version and others favouring a burnt flavour. These memories bring laughter and joy, and we hope you enjoy this as much as we do.

300g (10½oz) bakery-style stale white bread, such as baguette, ciabatta or sourdough – don't use regular loaves or sliced bread

1 litre (4¼ cups) milk

300g (1½ cups) caster sugar

5 large eggs, beaten

FOR THE CARAMEL:

250g (1¼ cups) caster sugar

TO SERVE:

dulce de leche (page 48), whipped cream or fruit coulis

You will need a large, non-stick Bundt tin or you could use two medium moulds or individual ramekins.

Start by making the caramel. Pour a small quantity of the sugar into a heavy-based frying pan, spreading it evenly to cover the base of the pan. Put the pan over a medium-low heat. Do not stir. As the sugar melts, add another 'layer' of sugar, allowing it to melt completely before adding more. Continue adding the sugar in layers and letting it melt each time so that it melts evenly and doesn't form lumps.

Once all the sugar has been added, stir continuously until the sugar turns a deep amber colour. Some people prefer the caramel to be 'burnt' for a bitter taste. If you like this too, just leave it for a few extra minutes for a darker colour. Quickly pour the caramel into the Bundt tin or divide it among two moulds or individual ramekins, swirling to coat the bottom(s) evenly. Allow the caramel to cool and harden.

Meanwhile, tear the bread into small pieces and put it in the bowl of a stand mixer fitted with the paddle attachment. Pour the milk over the bread and leave it to soak for 30 minutes.

Preheat the oven to 180°C fan (350°F fan).

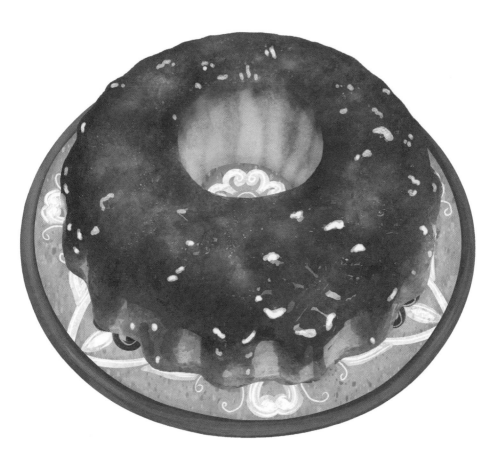

Once the bread has softened, add the sugar and eggs. Mix on a low speed for 2 minutes, until well combined. Pour the mixture on top of the caramel in the Bundt tin, moulds or ramekins.

Put the tin or ramekins in a large, deep roasting tin. Fill the roasting tin with water until it comes three-quarters of the way up the sides of the Bundt tin, moulds or ramekins. Carefully transfer to the middle rack of the preheated oven and bake for 50 minutes, until set. Remove from the oven, being cautious of the hot water.

Remove the Bundt tin, moulds or ramekins from the water and allow to cool for 30 minutes, then remove the pudding from the Bundt tin, moulds or ramekins by inverting each one onto a serving plate. Cut into slices and serve with dulce de leche, whipped cream or a fruit coulis.

CHOCOTORTA

SERVES 12

Chocotorta is a beloved Argentinian dessert that makes an appearance at every celebration. This rich, no-bake cake is made by layering Chocolinas, a traditional Argentinian chocolate cookie brand, with a dulce de leche and cream cheese filling. The cookies, which are crisp and slightly sweet, absorb the flavours of the filling as the cake chills, creating a delightful combination of a smooth, velvety texture and an intense chocolate flavour. It's funny how we all consider it to be a cake when it's really more of an 'assembly', in the words of Osvaldo Gross, one of the most respected pastry chefs in Argentina. The chocotorta was born from a marketing strategy to cross-sell the cookies with a popular brand of cream cheese in combination with the favourite Argentinian spread, dulce de leche. The recipe's creator, Marité, never thought it would be so popular.

FOR THE COOKIES:

200g (1²/₃ cups) plain flour, plus extra for dusting

180g (¾ cup + 4 tsp) caster sugar

70g (½ cup + 1 tbsp) dark cocoa powder

200g (7oz) salted butter, thinly sliced

60ml (¼ cup) milk

1 tsp vanilla extract

FOR THE FILLING:

800g (1¾lb) mascarpone cheese

100ml (¹/₃ cup + 4 tsp) cream

a splash of Baileys Irish Cream (optional)

800g (1¾lb) dulce de leche (page 48)

To make the cookies, put the flour, sugar and cocoa powder in the bowl of a stand mixer fitted with the paddle attachment and mix together. Add the butter and mix again until well combined, then pour in the milk and vanilla and mix until it all comes together into a dough.

Tip out onto a clean countertop and pat the dough down into a flat disc. Wrap with cling film and refrigerate for at least 30 minutes.

Preheat the oven to 180°C fan (350°F fan). Line two large baking trays with non-stick baking paper.

Roll out the chilled dough on a lightly floured countertop until it's about 5mm (¼in) thick. Stamp the dough into circles using a cutter with a 5cm (2in) diameter (or similar-sized squares or rectangles). Put the cookies on the lined trays, spaced slightly apart, and bake in the preheated oven for 12 minutes. Allow to cool and dry out on wire racks for at least 1 hour.

Meanwhile, to make the filling, clean the bowl and paddle attachment of your stand mixer, then put the mascarpone, cream and Baileys (if using) in the bowl and beat together until combined. Add the dulce de leche and mix again until combined into a light brown paste.

To assemble, remove the base from a deep springform tin and put the tin directly on a large serving plate. Add a layer of cookies, using as many as will comfortably fit in the tin. Cover the cookies with a layer of the filling about 1cm (½in) thick, then another layer of cookies and another layer of filling. Repeat the layers until you've used up all the ingredients or reach the top of your tin.

If you have any remaining cookies, crumble them and sprinkle them on top as a final decoration. Refrigerate the cake for 12 hours to allow it to set, then cut into slices to serve.

TORTA BALCARCE

SERVES 8–10

Two cakes are traditionally served at birthdays or other events: the Balcarce and the chajá. They are similar, but the chajá replaces the meringue nests with peaches. You can also swap out ingredients to create your own cake – for example, try using Nutella or raspberry jam instead of dulce de leche or add fresh strawberries. If you have a sweet tooth, no doubt you will come up with plenty of ideas!

FOR THE SPONGE CAKE:

butter, for greasing

200g (1 cup) caster sugar

6 large eggs

200g (1²/₃ cups) plain flour, sifted

1 tsp vanilla extract

FOR THE ALMIBAR (SYRUP):

55g (¼ cup) Demerara sugar

200ml (¾ cup + 4 tsp) water

FOR THE FILLING:

500ml (2 cups + 4 tsp) cream

60g (½ cup) icing sugar

100g (3½oz) meringue nests

500g (1lb 2oz) dulce de leche (page 48)

FOR THE TOPPING:

a handful of desiccated coconut, toasted (optional)

Preheat the oven to 180°C fan (350°F fan). Grease the base and sides of a 22cm (8½in) springform tin with butter and line with non-stick baking paper.

To make the sponge cake, put the sugar and eggs in the bowl of a stand mixer fitted with the whisk attachment and mix on a high speed for 4–5 minutes, until pale and foamy. Reduce the speed to medium and add the sifted flour gradually to avoid lumps. Once the flour has all been incorporated, add the vanilla and mix for another 2 minutes, until the batter is smooth.

Pour the batter into the prepared tin, spreading it out evenly. Bake in the preheated oven for about 30 minutes – a skewer inserted into the centre should come out clean. Allow to cool completely on a wire rack before you assemble the layers.

To make the syrup, put the sugar and water in a small saucepan set over a medium heat, stirring until the sugar has fully dissolved, then boil for 2 minutes. Allow the syrup to cool before using it to moisten the sponge cake layers.

To make the filling, whip the cream with the icing sugar until it reaches firm peaks, but be careful not to over-whip, as this can lead to a grainy texture and a buttery taste rather than the smooth, light cream you want to achieve.

To assemble, break the meringue nests into large pieces. You want them to stay substantial to provide texture.

Release the sponge cake from the tin and cut it horizontally into three even layers. Put the first layer on a large serving

plate and use a pastry brush to moisten it with one-third of the syrup, focusing on the edges. Spread half of the dulce de leche over the sponge, taking care not to tear it. This can be tricky because dulce de leche is so thick, so be patient! Spread half of the whipped cream over the dulce de leche, then add about half of the large meringue pieces.

Put the second sponge cake on top, then repeat the process for this second layer: syrup, dulce de leche, whipped cream and meringue.

Put the final sponge layer on top, moisten it with the remaining syrup and sprinkle over a handful of toasted desiccated coconut if you like, then scatter any leftover meringue pieces on top as decoration.

PASTA FROLA
QUINCE PIE

MAKES 2 PIES

Pasta frola is another example of how we adopted and embraced a recipe that can be found in Spain, Italy or Poland. This versatile quince pie can be enjoyed for breakfast, as a snack over mate or as a dessert. For this reason, it's widely available in bakeries and kioskos (shops where you can buy sweets, cigars and everything in between), where you can usually get it in individually wrapped portions. There are two classic versions of pasta frola: one with quince jam and another with sweet potato filling (additional variations include chocolate). Facu prefers the sweet potato version, but Pam loves both.

FOR THE DOUGH:

200g (7oz) salted butter, diced into small pieces

120g (½ cup + 1 tbsp) caster sugar

zest of 1 lemon

2 large eggs

400g (3⅓ cups) plain flour, plus extra for dusting

2 tsp baking powder

FOR THE FILLING:

700g (1½lb) quince jam

60ml (¼ cup) warm water

4 tsp cognac or brandy (optional)

To make the dough, put the butter, sugar and lemon zest in the bowl of a stand mixer fitted with the paddle attachment. Mix together on a medium speed until well combined and creamy, then add the eggs one at a time and keep mixing until well blended. Slowly add the flour and baking powder and mix until just combined into a dough, taking care not to overmix or your pastry will be tough. Form the dough into a flat disc, wrap it in cling film and refrigerate for at least 30 minutes.

Meanwhile, to prepare the filling, put the quince jam in a large bowl with the warm water and cognac or brandy (if using). Use a fork to loosen the jam and whisk it together with the liquid ingredients until smooth. This may take a few minutes, as quince jam is quite firm.

Preheat the oven to 180°C fan (350°F fan).

Divide the chilled dough in half and roll out each portion on a lightly floured countertop until it's about 5mm (¼in) thick. Using a 20cm (8in) loose-bottomed tart tin as a guide, cut out a circle that's a bit larger than the diameter of your tin. Save the remaining pastry scraps.

Carefully roll the pastry around your rolling pin, then unroll it over the top of the tin, pressing it down gently into the base and along the sides. Repeat with the other half of the dough and a second loose-bottomed tart tin.

TRY THIS

If you have any leftover dough and filling, you can make them into quince jam thumbprint cookies. Roll the pastry into small balls, flatten them slightly and make an indent in the middle with your thumb, then spoon in some of the filling. Put on lined baking trays and bake in an oven preheated to 180°C fan (350°F fan) for about 6 minutes, until golden. This cookie, known as a pepita in Argentina, is popular in bakeries and cafeterías.

Divide the quince filling between the two tins.

Gather up the pastry scraps, roll them out again until they are 5mm (¼in) thick and cut into long strips to form a lattice crust. This decorative pattern involves laying strips of dough over the top of the pie in a criss-cross pattern to create a woven effect. Or you can cover half of the pie with pastry strips and/or decorative shapes that you stamp out with a cookie cutter and leave the other half to show through, like we've done here.

Bake the pies in the preheated oven for 30 minutes, until the pastry is golden and the filling has set. Allow to cool completely on wire racks before removing from the tins and cutting into slices to serve.

BAILEYS TIRAMISU

SERVES 8–10

There are countless versions of this classic Italian dessert. While we are big fans of the traditional recipe, adding a bit of Baileys is a match made in heaven. But you can replace it with your preferred spirit, skip the booze altogether or even swap the coffee syrup for chocolate milk if you want to make it family-friendly.

FOR THE FILLING:

100g (½ cup) caster sugar

6 large egg yolks

3 tbsp water

700g (1½lb) mascarpone cheese, left out at room temperature for 15 minutes (don't let it get too warm)

200ml (¾ cup + 4 tsp) double cream

60ml (¼ cup) Baileys Irish Cream

FOR THE COFFEE SYRUP:

100g (½ cup) caster sugar

1 litre (4¼ cups) water

50g (2oz) instant coffee

60ml (¼ cup) Baileys Irish Cream

TO ASSEMBLE:

200g (7oz) ladyfingers

dark cocoa powder, for dusting

To make a sabayon, put the sugar, egg yolks and water in a large heatproof metal bowl set over a pan of gently simmering water (a bain-marie), making sure the water doesn't touch the bottom of the bowl. Cook over a low heat, whisking constantly to ensure it remains smooth, until the mixture reaches 85°C (185°F) on a candy thermometer or digital thermometer. Remove the bowl from the heat and set aside.

Fold the mascarpone into the sabayon. Be careful not to overmix, as this can cause curdling.

Put the cream and Baileys in the bowl of a stand mixer fitted with the whisk attachment and whip on a low speed, gradually increasing the speed over 8–10 minutes. Gently fold the whipped cream into the mascarpone mixture, then refrigerate until you are ready to assemble the tiramisu.

To make the coffee syrup, put the sugar and water in a small saucepan and bring to a boil over a high heat, then cook for 5 minutes. Remove the pan from the heat, add the instant coffee and stir until it's fully dissolved, then stir in the Baileys.

We like to assemble the tiramisu in a deep springform tin for a nicer presentation, but you could also use a deep baking dish. Start forming layers by soaking the ladyfingers in the coffee syrup for just 2 seconds, then putting them in the bottom of the tin or dish in a single layer and cover with a thick layer of the filling. Repeat the layers until all the ladyfingers have been used, ending with a layer of filling.

Dust the top generously with cocoa powder and refrigerate overnight (or for up to three days). Cut into slices to serve.

FERNET CON COCA

SERVES 1

Fernet con coca is one of Argentina's most iconic and cherished drinks – we even have songs about it. It's said to have been invented in Córdoba (one of Argentina's provinces), where it's called fernandito and is often served in a cut bottle of Coca-Cola.

The strong, herbal bitterness of Fernet balances beautifully with the sweetness of Coca-Cola, creating a cocktail that's refreshing, not too sour and not too sweet. Its digestive properties make it the perfect aperitivo, and while it packs a punch, it's known for not giving you a hangover if enjoyed in moderation. Traditionally served at asados, gatherings and celebrations, it's a cultural staple and a true symbol of Argentinian spirit, best enjoyed with friends and family.

3 ice cubes

2 tbsp Fernet-Branca

1 can of Coca-Cola

Put the ice cubes in a large glass. Pour in the Fernet-Branca, then slowly add the Coca-Cola, pouring carefully to minimise foam. ¡Salud!

INDEX

Nine Bean Rows

23 Mountjoy Square

Dublin, D01 E0F8

Ireland

@9beanrowsbooks

ninebeanrowsbooks.com

NINE
BEAN
ROWS

Blasta Books is an imprint of Nine Bean Rows Books Ltd.

@blastabooks blastabooks.com

First published 2025

ISBN: 978-1-7384795-7-3

Editor: Kristin Jensen

Series artist: Ciara Coogan
cicoillustrates.com

Designer: Jane Matthews
janematthews.ie

Proofreader: Jocelyn Doyle

Printed by L&C Printing Group, Poland

A CIP catalogue record for this book is available from the British Library.

For EU product safety concerns, contact us at our address above or info@ninebeanrowsbooks.com.

10 9 8 7 6 5 4 3 2 1

About the authors

Facundo Rodulfo and Pamela Neumann are the dynamic duo behind Tango Street Food in Killarney, Kerry. Their journey spans continents, bringing the flavours of their homeland, Argentina, to their new community in Ireland to foster cultural awareness and togetherness.

Facundo's passion for food began during childhood while watching his Spanish-Italian family cook Sunday meals. His uncle's founding of a pizza chain in Buenos Aires inspired Facundo to enter the culinary world.

Pamela's hospitality journey began at her parents' businesses, first a bakery, then later a hotel on the coast.

Once married, they managed the hotel and restaurant together before moving to Europe. Facundo participated in diverse gastronomic projects in Spain. Meanwhile, Pamela fell in love with Irish family culture while working in the travel industry. They moved to Kerry, drawn by its resemblance to Patagonia.

They started a food truck during the pandemic and now operate the first Argentinian restaurant in Munster and the only parrilla (open-fire grill) in Ireland. They enjoy visiting new destinations, trying different food and spending quality time with their four boys, who adore Messi and playing fútbol with their dad.

 tangostreetfood